CW01113166

WAVES

DHAMMA TALKS AND POEMS

By

BRIAN TAYLOR

COLLECTED BY LINDEN BROUGH

道

UNIVERSAL OCTOPUS

OTHER PUBLICATIONS

Blindness Kindness
Worm's Eye View
Going Out There is No Other
Coming Back There is No Trace
Blondin & Other Poems
Bamboo Leaves
Toi et Moi
Vienna
Basic Buddhism for a World in Trouble
Dependent Origination (*Paṭiccasamuppāda*)
The Ten Fetters (*Saṇyojana*)
What is Buddhism?
The Living Waters of Buddhism
Buddhism and Drugs
Basic Buddhist Meditation
The Five Buddhist Precepts
Centre: The Truth about Everything
The Universal Octopus & Mr Tao
Oxford Blues
Gnomonic Verses
Buddhist Pāli Chants and English Translations

Published by Universal Octopus 2017
www.universaloctopus.com

COPYRIGHT © 2010 ARIYA

First Edition 2012. Second Edition 2017

A catalogue record of this book is available from the British Library.

ISBN 978-0-9956346-0-2

All rights reserved.

For James

CONTENTS

INTRODUCTION 1

MEDITATION 3

STOP 5

DON'T WASTE TIME 9

STRESS 11

UNPLEASANT MIND STATES 13

LETTING GO 15

THE SAMSĀRA 17

THE SHANGHAI JAR 20

PEACE 22

POISONOUS SPIDERS 25

PERMANENT CURE 27

THE UNHATCHED EGG 29

IT CAME TO MIND 31

AWARENESS 34

VISĀKHA-PŪJĀ DAY 36

ASMI MĀNA 41

SELF AWARENESS 43

TRAVELLING TOWARDS THE GOAL 45

STOPPING THE REACTIVE MIND	47
DIRECT EXPERIENCE	49
RIGHT UNDERSTANDING	51
UNSHAKEABLE LIBERATION OF MIND	54
MĀRA'S TANGLES	56
RIGHT VIEW	58
THE GOAL	61
PERSEVERANCE	63
THOUGHT CONTROL	66
THE FIVE KHANDHAS	68
AS A THING IS VIEWED SO IT APPEARS	70
KARMA	72
REBIRTH	75
PROJECTS	77
THE NOBLE EIGHTFOLD PATH	80
GLOSSARY OF PĀLI WORDS	81

Oh ye inheritors of immortal bliss,

hearken to this!

Guardians of the eternal fire,

if to higher truths you do aspire,

NOTHING needs building any higher.

THIS IS THE TRUTH.

INTRODUCTION

After the Buddha's Enlightenment this thought arose in him:

"This profound truth that I have discovered is difficult to understand, tranquilising and sublime, not gained by mere reasoning, subtle, and is visible only to the wise.

The world, however, is given to pleasure, delighted with pleasure, enchanted with pleasure. Truly, such beings will hardly understand the law of conditionality, the dependent origination of everything; incomprehensible to them will also be the stilling of all formations, the relinquishing of every substratum of rebirth, the fading away of craving, detachment, cessation, Nibbāna.

Yet, there are beings whose eyes are only a little covered with dust: they will understand the truth."

Thus the Buddha 'went down and talked to the waves – and many heard'. This was because over two thousand years ago in that part of the world (which today is known as India), civilisation had reached a high evolutionary level.

There were many mendicants and ascetics who had left the worldly life in search of Truth.

Today, civilisation is not at a high evolutionary level – it is in a Spiritual and Moral decline.

This booklet contains a sample of intuitive, spontaneous research.

The Projects, Poems and Talks support our treading of the Noble Eightfold Path* to Nibbāna, the end of all Suffering.

.....How Many Hear?

---

* See page 80

MEDITATION

*T*hose who need to meditate the most, don't, and those who do meditate, enjoy it.

Those who don't meditate, need meditation the most. The mind is master of such beings and takes them all over the place; constantly moving, constantly thinking, planning, worrying, remembering. It instigates words and actions that only *you* have to suffer the outcome of – not mind, it's gone, moved on to more activity.

What one discovers in meditation is that mind disappears. In moments of complete absorption, it disappears. In moments of joy and happiness, or when one gets a shock, or complete surprise, or fright, it disappears. In the higher mental states and Nibbāna, it disappears.

It is only a tool to be carried around and used when necessary.

It is a poor master, but makes a good servant.

Some are still completely controlled by this mind which one could not call a living thing. It is a cause and effect phenomenon, hurtling through time and space, quite mechanically.

One needs to take this seriously and begin the work, *now*, of learning to master this mind. Some have a lot of work to do, to bring this mind under control, to a state of peace and tranquillity.

*Mind moves
with the breath
which fuels this articulated doll
from birth to death.*

*What starts out as routine maintenance
for a puppet with entangled strings
develops to a share in the dance
of the dragon that eternally sings.*

*But first, the intention,
clear and well defined
for the retention
of the errant mind.*

STOP

*I*t is normal to describe things by calling them big or small, heavy or light, beautiful or ugly. Or by giving them names like tree, grass, chair etc. This is done in order to distinguish between things. It is a conventional normality.

These descriptions and names are seen all to be relative; it is this compared with that. Something can only be heavy when compared with something light. What is heavy now may be light compared with something else at another time.

These characteristics change and disappear but the underlying characteristic remains unchanged. It is like a wave in the water. When there is movement, there is the wave. But when the water becomes calm and still, the wave disappears. What made up the wave does not disappear, it is still the sea. Nothing is lost.

This is what happens with Death. What makes up the being is karma, activity of body, speech and mind. When the movement ceases, the being ceases and the underlying characteristic returns to Source.

With Birth, it is the beginning of movement, activity of mind and body. The actual experience of this activity is felt in beings as suffering. The more active they become, the more propelled by karma, the more suffering ensues.

Everything begins with the same underlying flow of

movement. Through activity, the characteristics constantly change so that it becomes difficult to see any relation between this and that.

Or to see that, when stripped of its changing characteristics, as soon as the movement ceases, the thing to which a description had been applied, disappears.

Yet, nothing is lost, because the essential something, now without activity, was there before movement (Birth) and after the cessation of movement (Death).

The One and the many.

One: stillness. And when it fragments into movement, the Many.

Because of this, beings suffer and Buddha calls this the First Noble Truth: The Truth of Suffering. Because beings suffer, they seek to return to the One. But you cannot go to One as though it were a separate thing in a different place. To rediscover the original state of calm and tranquillity, you have to stop.

Very few can stop when they philosophically understand this.

The Buddha saw this and to overcome this problem of eternal activity, restlessness and suffering, he created the Noble Eightfold Path.

This Path gives clear instructions on how to tame and normalise one's activity so that one can calm the mind and stop it at will. A return to the original pure state of non-suffering is the result.

> *Pulled by the strings*
> *of the six senses*
> *going every which way,*
> *the uncontrolled puppet.*
>
> *Watch it.*
> *And listen to it.*
> *Stop it.*
> *And control it.*

*The Serpents dance hypnotically
and fill the Void with Thought
and in their game of wish-fulfilment
the Sons of Man are caught.*

*Slaves to their Dream Creations,
enflamed by Hot Desire,
craving ever-new sensations,
singed by the Ancient Fire,
they sink from brightness into embers
from cinders into dust,
with which they fashion ever-new contenders
for their never-cooling Lust.*

*In their high empyrean mansions,
the Masters watch and pass down
from Perfect Peace –
Living, trans-sangsāric ladders
for the burning souls' release.*

DON'T WASTE TIME

Not wasting time is a relative thing. It's not a waste of time for a soldier to practise shooting. It's not a waste of time for a gardener to dig his garden.

There are two things that are not a waste of time for *all* beings. The first is *survival*, and the second is *happiness*.

Beings would rather survive and be miserable than not survive at all; but most would prefer to survive *and* be happy. The happiness that most spend time chasing is short term happiness because whatever has caused it does not last, is not permanent.

It is better to spend time pursuing Spiritual Happiness which is long term - Eternal.

However, what is true of both kinds of endeavour is the danger of wasting time, letting the mind wander, letting it go wherever it likes.

The mind needs constant monitoring and, if not mastered, it wanders about like a horse with reins loose.

Good karma will produce pleasant daydreams and wanderings. Not such good karma will produce unpleasant thoughts and unpleasant destinations. Mostly we experience a mixture of the two.

To let the mind wander is a waste of our precious time.

Who controls the reins
the horse or the rider?

The puppet of a thousand strings
or the mind inside her?

Who impels the mind?

The smile
on the face at the front
or the ghostly fingers behind?

Who pays the piper
calls the tune.

But he who dines alone
picks up the bill.

STRESS

*T*he snow melts high up in the mountain and, if unimpeded, the water takes the most direct route to the sea.

If something gets in the way and stops its natural flow, a lake forms and spreads out in all directions, damaging things on its way.

Blocking the mind in its flow is felt as stress, tension and pressure. It builds up until it bursts out in a nervous breakdown or damaging behaviour through thoughts, words and deeds.

If the mind is like a Shanghai jar that has no bottom, it doesn't matter how much water is poured into it, it will never fill up. However, if there is a bottom to it, the water will build up until it overflows or bursts out.

Who will restrain her?
Who can contain her?
She dances in the wind
and drags her thousand thousand
children in her wake.

*Every time
I wind the clock
its ticks and chime
give me a shock.*

*And when this goes on constantly
it almost drives me mad!*

*If someone
would please STOP it
how glad I'd be!
How glad!*

UNPLEASANT MIND STATES

No one wants unpleasant mind states. Yet, if someone was wearing a black hat and saying, "I don't like black hats", we would wonder why he didn't just take it off.

It's the same with these unpleasant mental moods, why does one hold on to them?

Because it means giving up the really pleasant aspects that lead to the unpleasant and beings are not prepared to give up the pleasant.

The pleasant begins with the peaceful, happy mind flowing out through the sense doors, towards the impermanent, suffering, non-self – sense objects.

Each man his prison makes

in his own way,

inherits what he takes

and keeps his peace at bay.

*Journeying from the beginning
(of which there is no beginning),
travelling for millions of years
(which cannot be measured in millions or years),
I have come
and go on.*

No stopping.

*Just the onward movement
into the illimitable.*

Forever.

*No need to blame the wicked,
their shadows are at their heels.
No need to fear for the good,
haloes of light enclose their splendour.
No need to talk of escape,
escape from this prison
is a doorway into the prison yard
and back again.*

*This prison is <u>moving</u>
and all encompassing.
There is nothing outside it
to be escaped into.*

*There is no escape <u>from</u>.
There is only <u>stopping</u>.*

*Where there is stopping,
how can there be movement?
If there is no movement,
how could there be a prison?*

LETTING GO

*T*he caterpillar only lets go of its leaf when it sees a better leaf. It's the same with us – we only let go of something when we find something better.

If that 'better' was found in meditation by reaching at least the first jhāna, this would immediately enable a greater detachment and letting go of worldly things.

This is something interior, not of the world.

People who do a lot of grasping after things of the world are empty inside. They try to make up for this in the external but this never fills the emptiness.

We should all strive to attain, at the minimum, the first jhāna.

Where it is thought that treasure lies

the mind is drawn because of ties.

Where the treasure is not a thought

no mind is born and nothing sought.

Livingness,
held in place,
projects the image of a face.
The face itself no more form has
than moon on water, or shade on grass.
And yet fathers forth tears and laughter,
a story of before and after,
which sports itself upon Life's waters
until the blood-beat rhythm, strangely, falters.

Then tears and laughter, livingness and face
stumble here and lose their place.
And all things human are here unmanned
at the granite doorway into no-man's land.

Say, at this parting of the way
where all things hurt you,
what have you learned to pray
that will not desert you?
Here, where you find you are quite deaf and dumb,
what home-made lifeboat
have you made / become?

SANGSĀRA

*I*t's true that there must be an energy that keeps the sangsāra going and drags us along in it. This energy is sub-conscious. It takes the form of craving, grasping and ignorance. Every sensory contact feeds this energy, fuels the āsavas.

The three *āsavas* that it fuels are: -

> *kamāsava* ~ the sensual pleasures of tastes, sounds, sights, smells, touches and thoughts.
>
> *bhavāsava* ~ always wanting to become something.
>
> *avijjāsava* ~ not seeing, not knowing.

These cloud the clarity of the conscious mind and, because of this, karma is created.

It is the 'horse and rider'. The 'horse' is this wild, untamed sub-conscious. It is a very old part of the mind and filled with latent tendencies from past lives and all our yesterdays. The work is to train the 'horse'. This is difficult, but it must be done.

It is urgent because we don't know when we are going to die. If the 'horse' is not tamed, who knows where it will gallop off to – for another rebirth. Left to themselves horses wander off to where *they* want to go, not where the rider wants to be.

This training is easier when something is young, a colt, a puppy, a child. But the mind is *not* young, it's very, very old. This is why the training of it is so difficult.

The fretful tiger in a rage

prowls the confines of his cage.

Do not feed him. Pass him by.

And, of himself, he'll surely die.

*Leaks spill
from imperfections
in the core
and flood the mind
with passions.*

*The mind's frail shell
is permeable
and the urge to know and feel
pushes its tentacles
through sight and hearing, touch and smell.*

*Through these the passions spill
and overflow
to fill
that outer world
with action and reaction,
ebb and flow
and mingle there
as part of the blazing beacon
of despair.*

THE SHANGHAI JAR

A monk used the image of the 'Shanghai jar' to illustrate the calm and detached mind that doesn't get disturbed by anything.

He said that there were two kinds of detachment.

The first is obtained by using a scoop to empty the Shanghai jar. Because it has a bottom, when one tires of scooping out the water, it will fill up again.

The second kind is attained by removing the bottom of the Shanghai jar. Whatever is put in, or flows in, passes right through and doesn't get trapped and accumulate.

The bird leaves no tracks in the sky

nor does the passing butterfly.

The man his burden drags behind,

the products of his restless mind.

*Products of the Past
are apparent all around us.
All of them outlast
and eternally surround us.*

*But the Past for its own sake
is always out of view,
following in the wake
of something always new.*

*Looking for the Past itself,
records are all you find -
a fossil, video, compact disc
or fragment in the mind.*

*Mental facsimiles
images and thought,
shadows of eternity,
the wave of becoming caught.*

*Grasping after shadows,
nets emptiness and pain.
Freedom, it then follows,
means letting go again.*

PEACE

*T*he first kind of peace can be experienced when everything is going well in our lives.

We are liked and loved. We live in an agreeable place. We have enough money to satisfy our needs. We are respected at work. Our health is good and so on...

The test is when our loved one stops loving us, our friends let us down, our agreeable place is invaded by difficult neighbours or even war, we receive a phone call from work telling us that we are redundant... How many can maintain peace in the face of changes of this kind?

Other ways that support and maintain the first kind of peace include closing out the world, shutting down the senses. Some of us have put a lot of effort into this kind of peace. But at some point the impressions get in and set off reactions that disturb our peace.

It becomes obvious that it is something *inside* us that reacts.

These reactions induce unwholesome states of mind like envy, jealousy, anger, greed, impatience, frustration etc.

If the reaction could be de-activated, then the sensory impressions would just flow through the 'Shanghai jar' and out through the bottom. No unsatisfactory mental states could arise and that would mean the end of suffering.

What is this something inside us?

It is desire that arises as a result of wrong view of the sense phenomena. Though we can note the desire and resultant mind states, and antidote them with the Brahma Vihāras, this results in only temporary peace.

The Buddha says as things are seen, heard, thought or known, just let them be as they are seen, heard, thought or known *at that moment.* When you see, you just see. When you hear, you just hear. When you think, you just think and when you know, you just know.

Then you will arrive at an understanding that the sense objects that you perceive, have nothing to do with you. When you don't grasp after sense objects that you perceive, they will get no foothold on you. When you lose your foothold on the objects of sense, your mind and body will neither be in this world, nor in any other world.

This not being anywhere in both worlds means the *end of suffering.*

> *A peaceful day can cope with me.*
> *But can I cope with a peaceful day?*

*Freedom from the Past
is the Present.
Freedom from the Future
is the Present.*

*The Present
is a crack that runs
through the universe.
Into it everything disappears
like snowflakes
in a raging furnace.*

*For most people
the Present
is a mental space
filled by memories of the Past,
thoughts of the Future,
sense impressions
and a random stream of thoughts.*

*In the gap between thoughts,
the real Present can be seen;
like the sun at noon
through dusty cobwebs
BLAZING
in a clear sky.*

POISONOUS SPIDERS

*T*here are various degrees of ill will. From a slight irritation, a feeling of dislike, right up to full-blown anger and murderous hatred.

These 'poisonous spiders' arise as a result of sense contact. Something is seen, or heard, or thought. There has to be an object. When the object arises, so does a subject. This subject is the sense of 'I'. It is *asmi māna*. *I am* angry. *I* dislike *you*. *I am* angry with *you* (or some other outside phenomenon).

Now, a practising Buddhist just sees anger as a mental state. Simply label mind states correctly. No need to introduce a subject and object.

By *labelling it correctly,* it will subside. It will not move into taṇhā, upādāna, kamma, saṅkhāras and new khandhas.

This makes all the difference. This will *uproot* asmi māna. It is clear that we find this difficult.

Spirit is the substance of Happiness.
It cannot be perceived by Mind or Body.
It infuses them
when there are no fences facing.

*The Gardening Book
shows each picture with a label.*

*So that, when you look,
you will be able*

*to distinguish that which feeds
from common WEEDS
and plants that grow from POISONOUS SEEDS.*

*As for the garden, if you want to IMPROVE it,
if it's a weed, don't just name it,
go on and REMOVE it.*

PERMANENT CURE

Those who have lived a religious life in the past will have had the opportunity to suppress unwholesome mind states. But, over a period of time, suppression results in the build-up of a force that will erupt at a time when conditions are favourable to activate it.

Buddhism offers a permanent solution to this.

The suppression of these mental states of anger, ill will, resentment and so on, can manifest in body illness and pain.

The Noble Eightfold Path can produce the four stages of Sainthood that permanently remove negative states of mind.

Right view is the permanent cure,

guiding self back to the boundless heart pure.

*Flaws upon a face;
each indicates a place
where pain and sorrow grew
as an eddy of death-in-life flowed through.*

*Monitor the mind
that scatters the leaves the wind destroyed.
Monitor the mind
that blows its dead selves through the Void.*

*Each imperfection
is a recollection
of where unguarded thoughts
have left their mark;*

*a clear reflection
(in a dusty mirror)
of a deep and dazzling Dark.*

THE UNHATCHED EGG

*T*he three layers of the 'Unhatched Egg' are: -

- *Grasping after sensual objects* through seeing, smelling, hearing, tasting, touching and thinking.

- *Holding on to viewpoints* as all viewpoints create a barrier, except for the Four Noble Truths.

- *Belief in self:* thinking that I am my body and mind.

Extinguishing belief that body is self is the state of a Stream Enterer, Sotāpanna – the first stage of Sainthood.

The 'shell' of the unhatched egg is present in the moment to moment continuum - it is the flow of everyday life.

Are you a nut or a shell?
Inner seed
that germinates and grows
into the Tree of Life?
Or outer shell,
which, having fulfilled its purpose,
is food for compost heap or fire?

*If stopping were easy,
a thought beam
properly directed
would thread silently
through atom after atom
and bring the entire universe
to a standstill.
An empty mirror
reflected in itself.*

*If stopping were difficult,
the spider mind would jumble on,
piling thought on thought,
trapped in its own web;
threads spreading out in all directions,
atoms, like so many jostling beads,
dancing and tangling in ever clashing patterns,
keeping the entire universe
in eternally pulsating chaos.*

*The many-headed monster glaring
at its own reflection.*

*Not easy.
Not difficult.
A judicious response
to the Problem of Pain.*

*A letting go of all phenomena.
Again.*

IT CAME TO MIND

*I*s there a Sentry at the Mind door? Who is the Captain giving orders to the Sentry?

Is it Māra or Buddha?

Those of us who have not grown up in a Buddhist culture have difficulty with faith in the Buddha. We have been encouraged to make decisions for ourselves using our own intelligence.

This intelligence is infiltrated with the passions, moods, feelings and thoughts of our conditioning.

It has become Māra's territory.

Proper faith in Buddha and the Path is the antidote to having Māra as the Captain who gives orders to the Sentry.

You put your head

in Mara's noose.

It's up to you

to get it loose.

*A poem
opens a window
in the prison wall.*

*If it's not a poem
it is just a picture
on the wall.*

*Who paints pictures
on the prison wall
is surely in the gaoler's pay.*

*MAY ALL BEINGS BE HAPPY!
MAY THEY BE FREE FROM ILL WILL!
MAY THEY BE FREE FROM ENMITY!
MAY THEY BE WELL AND HAPPY ALL THE TIME!*

*When friendliness puts in an appearance
the starting place is non-interference.
Let the uncaged linnet sing.
Leave the butterfly on its wing.*

*When friendliness puts in an appearance,
MĀRA grasps its outward form
and wears it as his own disguise
with which he can his tricks perform.
He chooses
it to make him friends.
He uses it
to blind their eyes
and so accomplishes his ends.*

*He puts out bait for fish to find.
He leaves the snare to catch him birds,
sows seeds of craving in the mind
and mixes poison with his words.*

*And all the while
he threats and smiles.*

*BEWARE THE SMILER WITH THE KNIFE
WHO WANTS YOUR MONEY <u>AND</u> YOUR LIFE!*

AWARENESS

The lesser-developed beings try to deal with awareness by changing their environment. At a higher level, they try to numb awareness to dreamless sleep, using drugs, like barbiturates, or alcohol. The more advanced try to deal with it through concentration.

None of these deals with awareness itself. They are just ways to dull it down, switch it off, cover it up. They are temporary measures and give only temporary relief – the problem remains unsolved.

The awareness is of feelings, thoughts and perceptions.

Those well advanced on the Buddhist Path can deal with awareness of mind from a happy, peaceful viewpoint and are therefore able to maintain awareness.

Those who are not so far along the Path cannot maintain a happy, detached state of mind. They get swept away by thought. Their state of mind is often unhappy and thus a vicious cycle is perpetuated.

The longer the journey,
the more baggage you take.

(The more baggage you take,
the longer the journey).

Looking with dispassion,
with equanimity,
with detachment,
doesn't it shine brighter than a thousand suns?
And in every minute particular?
The broken wing
the severed finger
the uncompleted life
'the smyler with the knife'
the loss of all things dear
the smell of fear
spirochaetes, viruses and germs
and the ever-chewing sepulchral worms?

And don't we see a thousand times and more
that what we build up and try to hold in place
disintegrates and vanishes without trace?
And what we hoard up
and try to store
provides a breeding ground for rats?

And this which is the Past
is also Evermore.

What we cannot preserve here
we save for heaven
taking our joys and pains
across the no-man's land of death
(when we have felt the betrayal of the breath)
and there,
in finer, subtler, intellectual realms,
plant our standards;
and still the Eternal, empty wind
will blow them down.

VISĀKHA-PŪJĀ DAY

There are supposed to be more Buddhists in the world than any other religion. There are Buddhists in China, Japan, Burma, Ceylon, Thailand, Vietnam, Tibet, Indonesia, Russia and growing numbers in the democratic countries of Germany, France, Britain, U.S.A., Australia. There are even Buddhists in Greece.

The only places where Buddhists are not found are in Islamic countries.

This Buddhism that ripples through the world today began over two thousand years ago, as a result of a single event – the enlightenment of a human being in a particular place, under a Bo tree in Bodhi Gaya, Northern India.

It would be difficult for a Buddha to find a suitable place for the attainment of enlightenment and the teaching of it in the world today. But over two thousand years ago, in that particular part of the world, civilisation had reached a favourable level. There were many mendicants and ascetics who had left the world in search of Truth.

The Buddha came from a good family. This is a great help for all those who respond to and practise the Dhamma. It means that one is physically fit, sufficiently intelligent, with good morality and reasonable health.

The Buddha experienced, as a young man and heir to a small kingdom, what all young people experience momentarily at a certain point in their lives. Discontent. Even with wealth, education, status and family – with the best that life could offer, the Buddha was not content.

He felt there had to be a higher truth than a life of sensual enjoyment that at any time could end with death, or be interrupted by sickness and old age.

He looked around and saw only unsatisfactoriness in life. He also saw an ascetic who had renounced the world to find a higher truth.

In our country today, it is not easy to see an ascetic. The few monks that are around are shut up in monasteries. It is difficult for young people today, who have experienced this crisis of viewpoint, to see examples of others who have had the same doubts – and chosen another path.

The Buddha practised asceticism for several years but did not find enlightenment, even though he was recognised as having attained all that it was possible to attain, by the methods of the time. He found that the body only became weak and ill and close to Death. He decided to take the middle way of moderation in eating and concentrate on control of mind instead of body.

He remembered some mental states he had attained as a young boy and wondered if they were the way to enlightenment.

On the Full Moon Day of May, he sat down under a Bo tree to work with Mind. He was able to control the mind by entering states called jhānas. These sharpened and brightened the mind so that he could use his mind to investigate truth.

What he found was that as he contemplated on the phenomena that arose at the six sense doors – they disappeared! Everything *noted* at the six sense doors, when noted, disappeared, to be replaced immediately by new phenomena, which also disappeared.

He saw that everything had the three signs of impermanence, unsatisfactoriness and non-self.

From this clear seeing, the Four Noble Truths were seen. If one grasps after *any* phenomenon, one is viewing it as permanent, worth grasping so therefore satisfactory, and as having something to do with *I-Me-Mine*. This is a wrong view of reality.

Because of this grasping one suffers.

If there is no grasping, there is no follow-on suffering. This is the Third Noble Truth – the cessation of suffering, Nibbāna.

The Buddha could have stopped there. This is where Pacceka Buddhas stop and probably most Arahats. But what he did was to create the way, a Path leading to this realisation of the cessation of suffering, or Nibbāna, for all beings – the Fourth Noble Truth.

This Noble Eightfold Path, as it is called, is comprehensive and covers all aspects of living for a human being, whether layman or monk. It is guaranteed that anyone who follows this Path diligently, without deviation, will reach the realisation of Nibbāna, just like the Buddha.

What is the effect of this clear seeing of reality? It means that one has come to the end of grasping after any phenomena. This includes grasping after another body.

Thus, one knows clearly for oneself that the end of rebirth has come about. One 'dies', while still alive, to the mental activity that fuels a new rebirth as anything!

This is the end of suffering.

It is mind liberated from Death, Old Age, Sickness and Birth.

It is a state of Eternal Peace and Happiness.

The Sun shines

in a bucket of water

and doesn't

get

wet.

*In the dark tabernacle,
a shaft of sunlight
illumines the heart
and shines through
a million years of dust.*

*Clouds and clouds of swirling
dust
spiralling
through the light
which spills in a golden pool
on damp, grey stone and rust.*

*When the light moves
it does not take the dust there to it.
When the dust slides into darkness,
the light does not pursue it.*

*Why then does the heart invent
burdens to shoulder?
(Why does the heart consent
to the illusion of growing older?)*

ASMI MĀNA

*I*t is a very old and long root. It is difficult to spot because of its subtlety.

If one had arrived at an Ashram, and this wasn't spotted, one would be given a free rein to get on with one's practice. But if this root is spotted, one needs to practise some kind of karma yoga to root it out or at least diminish it.

Stalin's time in labour camps was his opportunity to root out something similar, but he wasn't there long enough.

It is the desire to have a role, to be somebody. The āsava of the desire to become – *bhavāsava*. From this arises asmi-māna – the 'I AM' conceit, ego-conceit, which may range from the coarsest pride and self-assertion, to a subtle feeling of one's distinctiveness or superiority. These feelings lead to attachment and culminate in clinging based on ideas of '*Me*' and '*Mine*'. Such attachments and involvements are what give rise to one's endless problems and difficulties.

Some beings with this root, when they discover that there is nobody, no self, are not liberated. They just lose interest in everything (because 'everything' had been a prop for their ego). They suffer from grief and sorrow and just die.

*The best way of enough is all gone
for that there is no argument upon.*

*While there is still something in the dish
there is in MIND propensity to wish.*

*Wishing is a film that spreads itself like jam
and turns the dullest pebble into a fragment of '<u>I AM</u>'.*

SELF AWARENESS

Self-awareness needs to be taken very seriously. One needs to be aware of self all the time, so that self can be changed, improved, modified and perfected. Without this awareness there is no possibility of change.

The time-tracks of most beings are full of wars, killing, bombs, and feuds. It is difficult for them to become self-aware – it's just too awful.

Those who can begin to have some self-awareness need to be open to self-correction from friends so that they don't put up the barriers of the old defence mechanisms of resistance, forgetfulness and self-justification.

The journey of Buddhism will never end if one tries to adjust the rules to suit oneself. If one continually wanders off the Path, and resists being told, it creates a deformity. An over-exercised right leg and a spindly, deformed left leg.

Buddhism is not for everyone. One may need to find another practice, or place. Though other religions are fine for those with different temperaments and aspirations, no other religion offers Nibbāna.

The phone rings at the mind door.
No need to wonder who is it for.

*Five golden chains
bind the painted puppet
(and restrain
and entrap it.)
Five wires hold it firm
and make it twist and dance (and squirm),
perform its tricks
(and for reward, receive its kicks).*

*Eye, ear, nose, mouth, skin
and one thick rope holds
(and controls)
the mind
within
(and keeps it blind).*

TRAVELLING TOWARDS THE GOAL

*T*rains are vehicles designed to journey to particular destinations. One buys a ticket for the place one wishes to travel to and boards the appropriate train. It should take you to the place marked on the ticket.

Buses, too, are vehicles for travelling to different destinations. Sometimes, a bus hasn't changed its destination label and is going somewhere else. We can be like that; we can pay lip-service to a goal but be acting in a way that leads to a different destination.

We need to be aware of what needs to be done, changed and corrected to be actually *sure* we are travelling towards the Goal.

It's easy to be distracted. Something might lead one just a little off the path. Other distractions can be huge and knock one off the path completely:

- know what you need to *avoid* and *overcome*.
- know what you need to *develop* and *maintain*.
- know that you are *making progress*.
- know what *hinders* you.

It's difficult for most people to be one-pointed. Their attention is always wandering. Off course and away from the Goal.

*Round and round the Circle Line
in endless pursuit of me and mine.
Familiar scenes go hurtling past,
each new vision much like the last:
grief and suffering, hate and pain
coming round again and again.*

*Where are the STOPS where the doors slide back
and offer a respite from the circular track?
Would I exit if I could?
Is there any choice but 'should'?
When the stations slide into view
<u>is</u> there a way-out for me? And you?*

*The train slows down and signs appear:
once more decision time is near.*

*CONCENTRATION puts an end to endless travel.
MORALITY helps the karmic tangles unravel.
TRANSCENDENTAL VISION unlocks the escape
hatch from this prison!*

STOPPING THE REACTIVE MIND

*T*here is one fundamental Buddhist tenet that must be understood and put into practice before any 'Unshakeable Liberation of Mind' can be attained and that is stopping the reactive mind!

Wherever one goes, be it monastery, cave, home, workplace, one will meet mind *reacting* to sense phenomena with feeling. In oneself and others.

Feeling must be understood as something separate and let go of, otherwise it is grasped hold of. Then attachments and aversions follow, creating desires, resentments, jealousy, envy etc.

These feelings come from *within* you and have nothing whatsoever to do with the phenomena that spark them off outside.

This must be understood and seen.

If you can't stop it,

Best jump off it!

*Why should the hand complain
for the glove abandoned in the rain?*

*Why should the foot retain
the ragged shoe and call it pain?*

*Why should the nerve-ends' loss and gain
reach any higher than the blood-filled brain?*

*The mind shines down from out of sight
to shine a shadow on a membrane.*

*But does not leave behind its light
or inflict on flesh a precious bane.*

*One arrow splits the skull in twain
but seeks to scratch the smile in vain.*

DIRECT EXPERIENCE

What will the mind be liberated from? The textbook answer is craving. But you need the direct experience of seeing this at work within your own mind.

When seen, it becomes fascinating and gives rise to many insights. Or it horrifies and one turns away and cannot investigate it.

Putting petrol on the fire

to douse the crackling blaze.

Like hounds, the latent tendencies rush on

in hungry pursuit

of the fruits

of the Second Noble Truth.

*Each tentacle that used to be anonymous
is now, by mutual consent, autonomous.
They may, at first, behave like fools,
but they'll get better as they learn the rules.*

*The Golden Rule shines brighter than the Sun:
one and one and one and one makes One!*

*The Suddenly Separate Spider Sentry
weaves his web and invites your entry.
But though he spins for ten thousand years,
all he catches is his own cold tears.*

*Fury and Deva goad the errant soul
to cleanse his vision and perceive the Whole.*

*The eddies of his mind are made of thought
and in their swirls many a shining world is caught.
But when the unhindered mind flows clear and free,
it knows itself to move most silently.*

RIGHT UNDERSTANDING

*R*ight understanding comes first. Without it, it is like the right hand pressing against the left. There will be exertion followed by fatigue. Exertion followed by fatigue again. Until one just gives up and wanders back into the forest to get lost in the jungles of sense pleasures.

Right understanding comes first.

Consider a butterfly; in the books they are given many different man-made names. But they *all* can simply be classified as 'butterfly' or 'insect'. We need to classify thoughts, feelings and perceptions in the same way. Instead of being ensnared in the details that make them different and losing sight of what they have in common, their sameness. We need to see that it is just these few things that make up our world, nothing else.

A thought is just a thought. A feeling is just a feeling – pleasant, unpleasant or neutral. Any more detail and one is lost in the world again. The associative mind grasps after the detail and we are lost in the tangle of thought, memory and imagination.

This is how *vipassanā* should be practised:

- *Seeing it is only thoughts or feelings that arise and pass away.*
- *Seeing that they have nothing to do with oneself and can lead on to suffering.*

This training in Right Understanding leads to detachment, a turning away from suffering and towards the Goal.

Do not follow the story line and wonder where the feeling came from and why. Of course, there will be a cause from the past but knowing this does not lead to liberation of the mind! It will draw one further into the tangles of the past.

Lift the screen and see the world,

the world you made as you passed by,

wrought with greed and raw desire,

your image carved in the sky.

*In the Jungle of the World
and the tangle of the Senses
we build us huts of mud and heartache
and make (and mend) our fragile fences.*

*"This is ME! This is MINE!"
is the burden of our song.
We cannot see, still less define,
that pain and sorrow prove us wrong.*

*This is NOT mine, this is NOT me,
is the beginning of our sanity.
Letting go of what does not concern us
leaves that alone which, meddled with,
will burn us.*

*The Law is mirror-like in its precision
and its simplicity needs no revision;
that Good breeds Good
and Evil has its price;
that Virtue is its own reward.
And so is Vice.*

*That all things pass away,
from butterflies to stars,
and though the World's a prison
it's the Mind that makes the bars.*

UNSHAKEABLE LIBERATION OF MIND

What is it that blocks unshakeable liberation of mind? Well, we have five senses – seeing, hearing, smelling, tasting and the sense of touch. And a sixth sense – mind, which is more subtle than the others.

The five senses allow us to have contact with the external world. Without them, it would not be possible. To make contact, there needs to be a sense (for example the eye), a sense object (something seen), and consciousness.

The mind's objects are thoughts, feelings, perceptions and consciousness.

The senses are neutral but because of ignorance, liking and disliking arise and an interior world is constructed based on thoughts, feelings, perceptions and consciousness. This leads to craving, grasping and attachment.

The result is suffering.

We have met the Buddha's Teaching in this lifetime. Let us attain the Goal – now. In this lifetime.

If we continually monitor the mind and stop it following thoughts, feelings and perceptions, eventually the work will be done – the mind will have achieved unshakeable Liberation.

Time drifts away,
as mist fades on the mountain.
The world itself is hardly more substantial.
The living water springing
from life's fountain
runs dry
leaving discarded bones
bleaching in the sun.

Molecules of arms and legs and brain
are rebels all and would be free again
and the whole pageant of our days and hours
runs only till we lose our feeble powers.

We are children playing out our days
with sandcastles and fantasies
until the turning of the tide slides in to erase
what we have worked so hard to raise,
struggled to protect and called our own –
fragments of things, at very best on loan.
Upward our thoughts might usefully aspire;
nothing down here needs building any higher.

Deal justly with your neighbour
and make of him your friend
and, in your inner garden, labour
until you reach your end.

MĀRA'S TANGLES

The butterfly is trapped in the spider's web. The more it struggles, the more entangled it becomes.

In our mind, what entangles us is grasping after the khandhas (*upādāna khandha*). Grasping after: -

- form
- feeling
- perception
- thought
- consciousness

Thus we are hopelessly entangled in Māra's net. In themselves the khandhas are neutral. It is we who grasp after them, from the moment of waking, all day long, until sleep, even into our dreams.

We must train ourselves to spot this and *not* grasp. It's not the khandhas that get caught in the net. It's not the khandhas that we are trying to liberate. It is mind.

The more I label
the less I am able
to see.
The more I see
the less I am able
to label.

*Speech
reaches out
to whisper and shout,
praise and curse,
across a silent universe,
making of molecular vibrations
a means for human communications.*

*It wasn't always quite like this;
groans and moans
hiss and howls
in warm Pre-Cambrian mud
were eloquent enough avowals
of love and hate and fear and blood.*

*Even now,
it isn't always quite the same;
grunts and lowing
of pig and cow
in farmyard barn and shed
make no poetic claim
but still express the cosmic suffering
of the living and the dead.*

*And when the fragile human mind
spirals downwards
and away from clear articulation
into the thorny tangles of sensation,
the fine distinction
of the human word
is dislocated and blurred
into the jabbering of animal and bird.*

RIGHT VIEW

*Y*ou have a wonderful opportunity now to use your time to study and investigate all phenomena until you reach realisation.

What comes first is Right View.

When this is firmly in place one will be well on the road to the Goal. However, any slight wavering in this will be reflected all down the line of the Path, becoming more noticeable in the more tangible speech and actions.

It is obvious that this is happening even with people supposedly high up in the Buddhist world. Their contemplation, investigation, has not been thorough enough.

The Buddha didn't encourage mixing in society while one is practising. He recommended remaining aloof from the world, in a cave, at the foot of a tree, in a solitary place. These provide suitable, undisturbed environments to work out one's salvation with diligence.

This investigation work is so subtle.

It requires solitariness. It can only be done by oneself.

If you don't like it Here,
bring it closer.

*Is stillness something
or is it merely
left over
when things disappear?*

*How can things
which are ever-moving
ever-changing
not be?*

*Stillness is complete and perfect
when boundaries disappear.*

*Cattle do not feel
the farmyard gate
pressing against
their outward-going faces.*

*The goat
does not feel the rope
tugging like the endless past
at its throat.*

*The bird does not break
its wing
against the window pane.*

*The butterfly does not
struggle into immobility
in the tangles of the spider's web.*

*The ear ceases to vibrate
the skin to be the terminus
of an electric field.*

*The eye is not stabbed
by arrows of fire.*

*When the sea is
a millpond,
a mirror to the sky above
a darkened window
to the hazy depths below
and the air palpable
in its stillness,
where have the waves gone?*

THE GOAL

Most people's goals fit into the space between Birth and Death. Relationships, families, houses, careers, possessions, wealth, power, fame. These are lost at Death, if not before.

The Buddhist Goal transcends Death. Permanent peace and happiness.

The Buddha clearly laid down what *needs* to be done and understood to reach the goal:

- We need to classify all phenomena as khandhas – to simplify all things into form, feeling, perception, thoughts and consciousness.

- We need to see how the mind flows out in pursuit of the khandhas continuously (*upādana-khandha*) and thus the mind gets caught in Māra's net.

- We need to find what practice enables us to stop the mind grasping – to stop the āsavas.

This is what needs to be *done* to have unshakeable Liberation of Mind.

"The goal of the Holy Life does

Not consist in acquiring alms,

Honour, or fame, nor in gaining morality,

Concentration or knowledge and vision.

The object of the Holy Life,

Its essence, its goal,

Is the unshakeable Liberation of Mind".

(Buddha: Majjhima-Nikaya: Sutta 29)

PERSEVERANCE

*T*here are two kinds of perseverance.

The first kind is perseverance within one's normal everyday life; including Meditation, study of Suttas, Dāna and Sīla.

The second kind is perseverance with mindfulness of the body and mind. To stop stirring the mind up. To let the mind settle just like muddy water in a bowl, the sediment sinking to the bottom. Perseverance is needed to avoid stirring it up and to allow the mind to settle into its normal, calm, peaceful and bright state.

Perseverance is to stop jumping on trains of wandering thoughts, feelings, memories, fantasies and so on.

It is not stirring the mind up.

It is letting go.

This second kind of perseverance is like being in a boat in the middle of a calm sea. Even in the calmness and peace, things will appear and try and jump into the boat. Perseverance must continue even in calm conditions, even after the 'storms' and 'stirrings up'.

One person on a see-saw can walk up one side. When he reaches the top, it's all downhill. Perseverance is like this. To begin with it's an uphill struggle.

The mind is very resistant to training.

But with continued perseverance with the difficulties and hindrances, one will make progress and reach the top.

From then on it's much easier, the perseverance becomes effortless now, and one just continues until the Goal is reached.

Holding a candle to drawn curtain,

shielding tired eyes against the sun.

Almost, but not quite, now half-certain

that one and one and one is One!

*Freedom
to fall
is a kind of freedom
that's common to all.*

*Freedom
to pain
when we hit the lower yard
again
is something that we all
find very, very <u>hard</u>.*

*It's all very galling.
you jump up off the wire
and find that falling
<u>doesn't</u> take you any higher!*

*You do not go
to become a constellation
but down below
to a very <u>different</u> destination!*

THOUGHT CONTROL

Something comes to mind. It comes again. It is persistent and keeps coming to the mind. Like someone persistently knocking on the door. Eventually, you give in to the desire. For the drink, the cigarette, something to eat, something to buy.

At first and for a little while the mind is appeased. But then the desire comes again. Another thought of the same kind, fuelled by the feeling of must. You give in to it. Again and again until it becomes an addiction. A compulsion. A habit.

A meditator has to deal with this and cure himself. He just notes the thought again and again until it stops coming compulsively to the mind. Then he can look at the thought and investigate it. Is it a wholesome thought? Is it something worth doing? Now he can, consciously, without compulsion, decide whether to act on it or let it go.

Only those who meditate can do this.

> *Paint a tiger*
> *on the wall.*
> *Turn and run*
> *(in case it catches you).*

*Full of danger is this world of ours
which threatens us on every side.
Floods and fumes and killers and cars.
These appear the whole world wide.
Constant vigilance is needed
just to keep oneself alive.*

*But the greatest danger
lurks within.
There lies the beginning
(and end)
of every single sin.*

*It is moral armour
that protects one,
from one's own karma.*

THE FIVE KHANDHAS

*T*he unique view of the world that the Buddha taught is that everything can be viewed in terms of five groups – the five khandhas: -

1) body (*rupa-khandha*)
2) feeling (*vedanā-khandha*)
3) perception (*saññā-khandha*)
4) habitual tendencies (*saṅkhāra-khandha*)*
5) consciousness (*viññāna-khandha*)

These khandhas can only arise on sensory contact through the six senses: -

eye ~ visual object ~ eye consciousness

ear ~ sound object ~ ear consciousness

tongue ~ taste object ~ tongue consciousness

nose ~ odour object ~ nose consciousness

body ~ tactile object ~ body consciousness

mind ~ thought object ~ mind consciousness

The arising of consciousness, as a result of sensory contact, sets off the khandhas of feeling, perception and thoughts. Only one can be present at any one moment but they are all intertwined and interdependent.

* *See saṅkhāra in the Glossary of Pāli Words.*

Ten thousand pieces on the floor
can reconstruct your own jigsaw,
each one shaped at the five sense doors
to compose the picture you are looking for.

The Alps with snowflakes? Fir trees? Chalets?
Figures skating down chasmic valleys?

Make no mistake. This mountainscape's not real
and only serves to cunningly conceal
the vision of Eternity that always comes too soon,
the dull and empty drabness of a Sunday afternoon.

AS A THING IS VIEWED SO IT APPEARS

Looking at a dog one might view a hairy animal with four legs, or a guard dog, or a family pet, or something to inject if one is a vivisectionist. As a thing is viewed so it appears.

They are all viewpoints which can submerge the truth - that a dog is a *living being* which suffers just like us.

This is the First Noble Truth.

It is Right Seeing and *not* a view from a particular standpoint, that of the observer. When the Truth is seen, the shift in viewpoint is spontaneous.

Then, through observation, the Second Noble Truth can be observed and investigated, followed by the Third Noble Truth and the Fourth Noble Truth.

These Truths are to be seen and realised by oneself to create the spontaneous adjustment to Right View which results in freedom from suffering.

Sitting on the spokes
he cannot see the wheel clearly
being part of the movement.

*Watching the flow
of middle-earth
as all things go
from birth to birth.
Here, one can know
what it's all worth.*

*An empty tide
of rise and fall.
Nothing outside
is mine at all;
-nothing <u>inside</u>,
nor large nor small.*

*The mind reflects
vague shadowy drifts.
The mind connects
blank mists with mists.
The mind projects
<u>meaning</u> – where none exists.*

*Rich and poor
in ragged procession
pass the door
and dispute possession
of what they cannot own;
like dogs, bemoan
an <u>imaginary</u> bone.*

*Ever so long ago. Today.
And ever-after.
Your tears will wash away
your broken laughter.*

KARMA

*K*arma means action, things done, doing. There is a connection:

- *Between an action and its consequences.* A good deed is one that produces a good result. A good tree is one that produces good fruit.
- *Between an action and the consequences for the doer.* Do good and get good. Do bad and get bad. Plant a good tree and you get good fruit.
- *Between an intention and the deed.*

If you intentionally give a poor man a pound, both of you benefit. If it falls out a hole in your pocket and the poor man finds it and picks it up, only he benefits. If you tread on a snail deliberately, you have created karma. The snail suffers. Because of your intention, you will suffer too. Somewhere. Sometime. If you step on it accidentally, the snail suffers. Because you had no intention to harm it, you may not suffer.

Moral purity protects you.

Nevertheless, even accidental actions can cause unsatisfactory karmic results for oneself. Suppose that instead of a snail, it had been the tail of a tiger. Would it have made any difference if you had said, "Sorry! I didn't intend to do that." Possibly not. Tigers are unpredictable.

The important thing is not to spend too much time

analysing the actions of others, but to monitor one's own actions carefully and honestly.

Guard your intentions.

Guard against carelessness.

This enables one to fulfil two of the three basic tenets of Buddhism:

- *Don't do evil*
- *Do good*
- *Purify own mind*

Purifying the mind is also governed by karma on the mental level. If one purifies one's mind, the result is greater clarity of mind and greater happiness.

Different kinds of karma carry different weight.

If I drop a cup on a hard floor and it doesn't break, I can put it back on the table. This is the type of karma that can be put right.

If I drop a cup on a hard floor and it breaks into pieces, it doesn't matter if I glue the bits together, it will never be the same. This is the type of karma that cannot be put right. All we can do is to live with the results until they have run their course.

A quarter to Now is far too late
to escape the shadow of your Fate.

*It's easier to chop down
an acorn
than an oak.*

*(The branch you bang
your head on
was an acorn
that you missed.)*

REBIRTH

Rebirth is not the same as reincarnation.

What gets born? The answer, according to the Buddha, is *nāma-rūpa* and it is nāma-rūpa that dies. In Buddhist understanding there is <u>no</u> entity, soul, spirit, or Atman, that is passed from one body to another. What passes on is *taṇhā* - craving.

The words 'I go', 'He is a monk', 'That is a policeman' etc, are used by followers of the Buddha with full understanding that they are describing the *'sammuti'* world of conventional reality – a 'let's make believe' or 'let's pretend world'.

What causes rebirth is the craving (*taṇhā*), the desire to become – the flowing out of the āsava, *'bhavāsava'*.

A child is <u>not</u> born.

It is created.

*There in the dark, waiting.
The unborn
seeking their opportunity,
moist earth
where they can flower
and be carried along
on the stream
of unfolding consciousness.*

*Only by constant vigilance
is the Bind Weed,
stored in the Dreamtime,
abandoned
to the stagnant backwater
of time –
to come no more.*

PROJECTS

One need never be without a Project of one's own. Any project that will help one overcome and remove a particular fault one has seen in oneself.

It's very difficult to see our own faults. It needs a certain level of mindfulness and awareness. This awareness must be in the moment of the fault arising – see it and stop it!

Mindfulness is the way to the Deathless, the Buddha said. He also said 'that those who are not mindful are as if dead already'. This is because they act automatically, like programmed machines, without any self-awareness at all.

Use mindfulness to remove faults and let there be serious progress. It would be a shame to miss Nibbāna after meeting Buddhism in this lifetime.

A lifestyle

that doesn't shut it's eyes

to the First Noble Truth.

Going out there is no other.
Coming back there is no trace.
Though we must still love one another,
whose is the beloved's face?

Start from wherever you think you wish to,
you cannot end up in a different place.
Scrutinise carefully the mirrors around you,
all that you see is the same old face.

Blame not the mirror for the malformation,
polishing the glass won't improve the skin.
If you intend a transformation,
smile with a smile that warms from within.

Snow bright eyes

Sunlight smiles

Spirit flies

One thousand miles

THE NOBLE EIGHTFOLD PATH
(ariya-aṭṭhaṅgika-magga)

1. RIGHT UNDERSTANDING
   (sammā-diṭṭhi)

2. RIGHT THOUGHT
   (sammā-saṅkappa)

3. RIGHT SPEECH
   (sammā-vācā)

4. RIGHT ACTION
   (sammā-kammanta)

5. RIGHT LIVELIHOOD
   (sammā-ājīva)

6. RIGHT EFFORT
   (sammā-vāyāma)

7. RIGHT MINDFULNESS
   (sammā-sati)

8. RIGHT CONCENTRATION
   (sammā-samādhi)

GLOSSARY OF PĀLI WORDS

Arahat: One who has got rid of ten fetters. He has realised Nibbāna in himself and will not be reborn.

Ten fetters:
1. Own body views.
2. Doubt.
3. Clinging to the practice of Morality.
4. Desire for sense objects and existence.
5. Ill will.
6. Desire for existence with forms.
7. Desire for formless existence.
8. Conceit. Pride.
9. (Mental) Restlessness.
10. Not seeing reality. Ignorance.

The first five bind to the lower worlds. The second five bind to the higher worlds.

See 'The Ten Fetters' (Sanjojana) ISBN 978-0-9571901-1-5

Āsavas: Desire for sensual existence. There are three: Desire for Becoming; Views and Opinions; Ignorance, not seeing.

Avijjā: Not seeing. Ignorance of the Four Noble Truths concerning Suffering; its Cause; its Cessation; The Way leading to its Cessation.

Asmi-māna: The conceit that I am (a separate entity).

Upādāna: Clinging; an intensified result of craving. Before one has something, one craves for it. When one gets it, one clings to it.

Brahma-Vihāras: Dwelling places of Brahma. Sublime (Divine) states of mind: Friendliness, Compassion, Sympathetic Joy and Equanimity. Together, they produce an attitude of mind towards all other beings which is wholly positive and beneficial.

Dāna Giving, generosity. A fundamental virtue and intentional practice.

Pāli: An Indo-European language related to Sanskrit in which the Buddha taught and in which the suttas were later recorded.

Paticcasamuppāda: Dependent Origination.

Avijjā forms the base for *Saṅkhāras*.
Saṅkhāras form the base for *Consciousness*.
Consciousness forms the base for *Mind and Body*.
Mind and Body form the base for the *Six Sense Bases*.
The *Six Sense Bases* form the base for *Contact*.
Contact forms the base for *Feeling*.
Feeling forms the base for *Craving*.
Craving forms the base for *Clinging*.
Clinging forms the base for *Becoming*.
Becoming forms the base for *Birth*.
Birth forms the base for *Old Age, Death, Sorrow, Lamentation, Pain, Grief* and *Despair*.

Dhamma: (Sanskrit Dharma)
    1. Things.
    2. The Buddha's Teaching. The Truth.

Khandhas: Groups, categories. The Buddha analyses our experiences into five categories: body, feeling, perception, saṅkhāras and consciousness.

Kamma: (Sanskrit Karma): Action; Doing. Specifically how all actions have a cause and an effect and the relationship between them.

Jhānas: Tranquil meditative states in which the mind is withdrawn into itself, free of the five senses.

Māra: The Deity ruling over the Highest Heaven of the Sensuous Sphere. He tries to keep living beings enslaved in sensual existence, tempting all those who try to go beyond this, so that they fall back within his realm. For the six years before Buddha's Enlightenment and one year after it, he followed the Buddha trying to find a weakness in him that he could exploit. He tried to persuade the Buddha to pass away into Parinibbāna without teaching the Dhamma. When the time came for the Buddha's Parinibbāna, he reappeared to urge him on. Immediately after the Buddha's death, Māra searched for some trace of him on earth and in the various heaven worlds without success.

Nāma-rūpa: Mind and Body. A Form and the Name given to it by humans.

Nibbāna: (Sanskrit Nirvāṇa). Every thing in the universe is a saṅkhāra. Nibbāna is not a saṅkhāra. Nibbāna is like the cinema screen. The universe is all the pictures and images superimposed on the screen. Because of the pictures, we can't see the screen. Yet it is there all the time. If we could clear the screen of the pictures, we would see it immediately. If we stop all sense perceptions and thoughts and images, Nibbāna is revealed. When we find the whole universe, mind and body, unsatisfactory, and let them go, they fall away from us and we experience total Peace and Happiness.

This is a state that has always been there. From time to time we get flashes of it. It is not death. Death is the end of something. Nibbāna is not the end of anything. It is a state without a beginning and without an end.

Sangsāra: The wandering on. The continuous process of being born, growing old, suffering and dying, in which beings are trapped. In its flow, they act and experience the consequences of their actions (Kamma). It embraces the whole spectrum of existence from the highest heavens to the lowest hells. Only the attainment of Nibbāna puts an end to the wandering.

Sammuti-sacca: Conventional truth. The whole fabric of our social lives as civilised or semi-civilised human beings and the roles we play in our public and private lives. As Shakespeare expressed it:

> All the world's a stage,
> And all the men and women merely players;

They have their exits and their entrances,
And one man in his time plays many parts......

So, we take up positions and play accepted parts in the social fabric, almost on a "Let's pretend" basis (which is what sammuti basically means). The parts are innumerable: policemen, teachers, politicians, doctors, carpenters, fathers, mothers, schoolchildren, labourers - even soldiers. Although if we choose to play at soldiers, we may find ourselves actually killing somebody; which suggests that the "game" might have got out of hand.

Saṅkhāra: Something which is made up of parts; a compound. Not an unchanging thing in itself. Everything in the universe is a saṅkhāra. For example, a motor car; the parts come together and it exists, we can drive it. After a while, the parts fall apart and are reused or decay or are destroyed and there is nothing left over. For example, a human being.

We give things names, but once they have disintegrated into their respective parts, there is nothing left over to correspond to the name.

Mental things are also saṅkhāras. Thoughts come into existence, based on perception, then they disappear. They form parts of trains of thought, which in their turn break up and vanish.

The sangsāra is made up of saṅkhāras. Just as the moving picture on the screen is made up of images of people, cities, trees etc.

Nibbāna is not a saṅkhāra, just as the screen is not in any way a part of the film and its images.

Saṅkhāras depend on Ignorance of the Four Noble Truths. Once the truth about suffering is realised, ignorance disappears. Just as when the screen is seen, we no longer believe in the reality of the film.

Sīla: Morality, right behaviour. The basis of morality is not causing suffering to oneself or others. Specifically, one should not do to other beings what one doesn't want to be done to oneself.

Sotāpanna: A "stream enterer". One who has entered the stream of activity which leads to Nibbāna. He has put an end to the first three Fetters.

Sutta: Discourse by the Buddha himself or certain of his leading disciples.

Taṇhā: Craving. The cause of suffering. Literally it means "thirst". If one thinks of the thirst of an alcoholic for alcohol, one gets some idea of the strength of the term. So long as there is craving for anything whatsoever, good or bad, one will always be motivated to enter into a form of existence where the object of one's craving can be found.

Upādāna-khandhas: Clinging to the five khandhas which make up the whole of a human being's life: body, feelings, perceptions, thoughts (sankhāras) and consciousness. Simplified, this means clinging to body and mind i.e. to individual life itself.

Vipassanā: A method of meditation. *One tries to make the mind aware of everything as it arises*

This is simple. It is not easy. If one can do it, one is face to face with reality itself, the actual continuous flow of one's life. If one perseveres, one comes, by degrees, to understand how everything works; how one's attention is caught by a sense perception and one is drawn towards it. How this outward reaching leads to actions through thoughts, words and deeds, which have consequences for oneself and others.

It is similar to focusing one's attention, minutely, on the detail of the images which appear on the cinema screen. If one can restrain oneself from being drawn into the story of the film, one comes to see that all these pictures, which succeed each other so rapidly, are none of them real; the fire is not hot, the water is not wet, the heroine is not a real girl. Becoming disenchanted with the illusion of it all, suddenly one sees the screen behind it. Similarly one has a sudden direct experience of Nibbāna.

Visākha-Pūjā: Visākha is the name of the sixth lunar month. On the full moon of that month, the Buddha was born, became enlightened and passed away into Parinibbāna (died). Pūjā means paying respects. The anniversary of this day every year is celebrated throughout the Buddhist world.

Lightning Source UK Ltd.
Milton Keynes UK
UKHW011843180619
344621UK00001B/3/P